W9-CYA-606

Usborne

# The Story of the Nativity

Usborne

# The Story of the Nativity

Anna Milbourne

Illustrated by Alessandra Roberti

Designed by Nicola Butler

Once upon a time, long, long ago,
an angel flew down from Heaven.

He went to the small, dusty village of Nazareth,
to visit a young woman named Mary.
Mary had never seen an angel before,
and she was very frightened.

"Don't be afraid, Mary," the angel said softly.
"God sent me to tell you that you're going
to have a baby boy. He is God's son."

Mary was not rich or important,
but she was gentle and good.
"I will do whatever God wants," she said.

Mary got married to a kind carpenter named Joseph.

When it was almost time for Mary to have her baby, a message came from the ruler of the land. Everyone had to go to the place their family came from to be counted.

Mary and Joseph had to go to Bethlehem, far away.

When they got there it was late,
and Mary was very tired.
She and Joseph walked through the
sleeping streets to find somewhere to stay.

But there was no room left anywhere.
When they came to the very last inn,
the innkeeper said, "I'm sorry. The only
place I can offer you is my stable."

That night in the stable,
Mary gave birth to a baby boy.
She named Him Jesus.

There was no crib for His bed,
so she wrapped Him up warmly
and laid Him in a manger full of hay.

Mary looked at the tiny baby
and she loved Him.

On the hills outside Bethlehem, a group of shepherds were looking after their sheep. Suddenly a bright light appeared in the sky. The shepherds trembled with fright.

An angel appeared, and said to them, "Do not be afraid. I am bringing great news. Today the son of God was born. You will find Him lying in a manger."

All at once the sky was filled with shining angels singing for joy.

They disappeared as suddenly as they had come, and the night was silent and dark again. One of the shepherds whispered, "Let's go and find Him."

They found baby Jesus
lying in the manger,
just as the angel had told them.

The shepherd boy wanted
to give the baby a gift, but he
was too poor to buy anything.
So he gave Jesus a little
woolly lamb.

Far, far away, three wise men saw a bright new star twinkling in the sky. "This is a very special sign," said one. "It means a new king has been born."

They followed the star
for miles across the desert
until they came to the stable.

The star hung over
the shabby stable roof.
Even though it was no palace,
the wise men knew they would
find the newborn king inside.

The three wise men went into the stable,
very quietly so as not to wake the baby.

They knelt before Him in the straw, and gave Him gifts fit for a king - gold, frankincense and myrrh.

And that was the very first Christmas.

Ever since then,
at Christmas each year,
people tell the story of how
baby Jesus came into the world.

Edited by Gillian Doherty

First published in 2009 by Usborne Publishing Ltd,
83-85 Saffron Hill, London EC1N 8RT, England.
www.usborne.com. 
First published in America in 2010. UE.